CARTOONS OF COERCION-II

THE ARISTOCRACY'S QUEST FOR POWER & WEALTH
BY FELTON WILLIAMSON, JR.

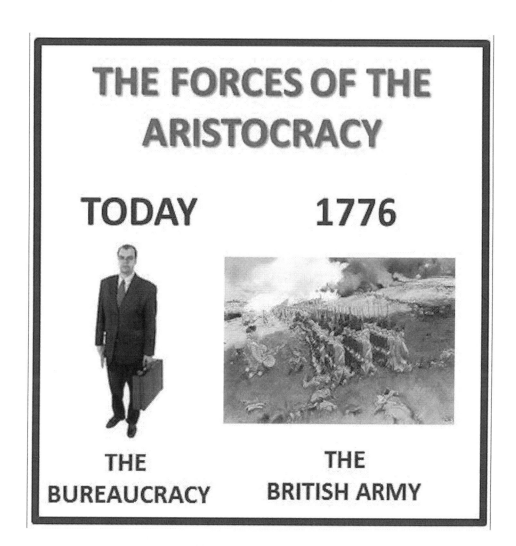

DEFINITION OF TERMS AS USED IN "CARTOONS OF COERCION-II":

"Aristocracy": those who would initiate the use of force against the individual in pursuit of wealth and power. The Aristocracy believes that control of the individual is necessary because the individual cannot be trusted to control his own destiny.

"Capitalist": advocate of individual freedom (Capitalism). One who opposes the initiation of force against the individual.

"Entrepreneur": the individual who uses his intellect and resources to facilitate the creation of wealth.

"Wealth": the goods and services required for the survival of a civilized society.

"Bipartisan": The opposition party joins the Aristocracy to pillage the Economy and quash the Constitution.

Because the meaning of the term Aristocracy is so important in this book, the definition from the Bing Dictionary and Encarta Dictionary is included.

The definition of Aristocracy from the Bing Dictionary:
- People of highest social class: people of noble families or the highest social class
- Superior group: a group believed to be superior to all others of the same kind
- Government by elite: government of a country by a small group of people, especially a hereditary nobility

The definition of Aristocracy from Encarta Dictionary:
- People of the highest social class. People of noble families or the highest social class
- Superior group: a group believed to be superior to all others of the same kind
- Government by the elite: government of a country by a small group of people, especially hereditary nobility
- State run by the elite: a state governed by an aristocracy

The history of mankind has been a struggle between Aristocracy seeking to impose their will on the Entrepreneur (innovator and producer of wealth) and control the wealth produced by the Entrepreneur.

ISBN-13: 978-1500705671
ISBN-10: 1500705675

DESCRIPTION of "Cartoons of Coercion-II":

Cartoons instead of tedious text make it easy for the reader to understand the Aristocracy's assault on individual freedom.

These cartoons display the motives, objectives, actions and consequences of the success of the Aristocracy in enjoyable illustrations. Recent action of the Aristocracy reinstating and exceeding the tyranny of King George III is illustrated with their disastrous results.

Each cartoon is listed in the table of contents so that the reader can quickly access any of the cartoons. In the Kindle edition, the reader can go to the "table of contents" and click on any cartoon title and the text page of that cartoon will be displayed.   This allows the reader to use the Kindle, Fire, computer, iPhone, iPad, or android to quickly make a point during a discussion or show the cartoon to a friend to start a conversation.

"Cartoons of Coercion" is composed of seventy-six cartoons and approximately 5,500, words so enjoy the pictures.

KINDLE V/S PRINT EDITIONS:

Because the Kindle edition must display illustrations on a small screen the print edition manuscript was unsuited to the Kindle format. It resulted in small illustrations and blank pages. Because of the Kindle's small screen, it is not practical to display text and the cartoons on the same page. The Kindle edition manuscript is necessary for optimum display of the cartoons on all the Kindle devices. In the print edition, the cartoon and text referring to that cartoon are printed on the same page.

Kindle Devices with a color display will show the cartoons in full color.

Table of Contents

The "Table of Contents" lists all illustrations and some text passages. The reader may go to any subject or cartoon by clicking on the title in the table of contents. This statement marks the end of the "Table of Contents."

PROLOGUE:

The Declaration of Independence, United States Constitution and the Bill of Rights amendments created a nation with individual freedom unique in recorded history. For a short time most individuals were a virtually free of coercion by the government and the results were prosperity and technological advances unequaled in man's history.

The United States Constitution is not a perfect document, but it was the best effort of the Founding Fathers based on the knowledge, customs and political reality of 1787. The Aristocracy's coercion of the individual and control of the economy was interrupted. It took almost 200 years of Aristocracy to reinstate a level of coercion and control of the economy exceeding the tyranny of King George III. The aristocracy used promises of unearned wealth, economic favors and security to exploit the flaws in the Constitution. Thus, the Aristocracy has accumulated the power and wealth they felt was their due.

In the beginning, the Aristocracy's progress of corrupting the Constitution was very slow. Immediately upon the ratification of the Constitution, the counter-revolution began. But the Aristocracy made very little progress until 1888. In 1888, the Bureaucracy was established by the creation of the Interstate Commerce Commission (ICC). The mechanism for application of the government's monopoly on force for the benefit of the politically powerful was established and in place. It's been downhill ever since!

"CARTOONS OF COERCION" is composed of cartoons exposing the corruption of the Constitution by the aristocracy. Amending the Constitution by reinterpretation has facilitated the insidious growth of coercion of the individual for the benefit of the Aristocracy. This is what the Aristocracy means when they speak of a "living breathing Constitution." The Aristocracy has achieved tremendous power and has even exceeded the tyranny of King George III.

A free and prosperous people are being converted into 21st Century Serfs.

The choice is between a Dictatorship (oppression) and a Republic.

LEFT OR RIGHT?
DICTATORSHIP OR REPUBLIC?

Commonsense21c.com

CAPITALISM V/S TYRANNY:

The cartoon displays the relationship between prosperity and freedom. History has shown that freedom begets prosperity. The graph plots prosperity v/s freedom.

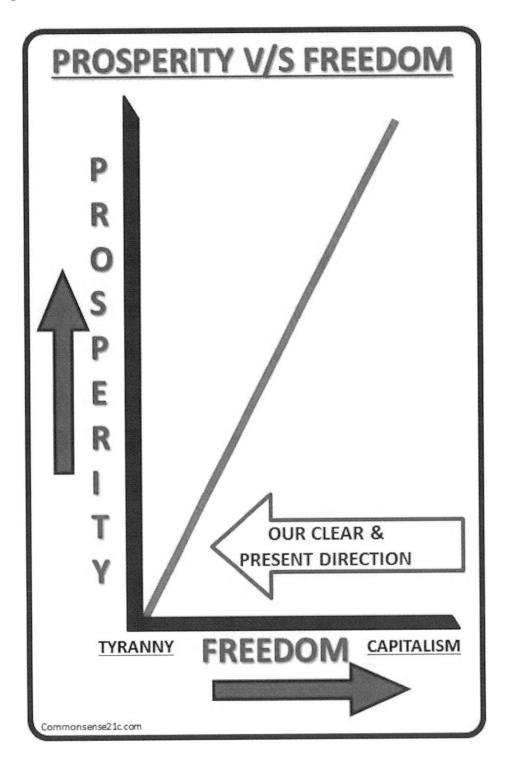

A LOGICAL DEFINITION OF THE POLITICAL SPECTRUM:

Conventional wisdom places Communism on the extreme left, Freedom in the center and Fascism on the extreme right.

Both Hitler and Mussolini were Dictators yet both claimed that Fascism (the name chosen for their brand of Dictatorship) was an alternative to Communism and Socialism, Hitler made this claim even though the name of his political party was "The National Socialist German Workers Party."

Logic dictates that the political spectrum consists of:

- Dictatorships and slavery on the extreme left
- The mixed economy, government coercion mixed with individual freedom in the center
- Capitalism, individual freedom on the extreme right.

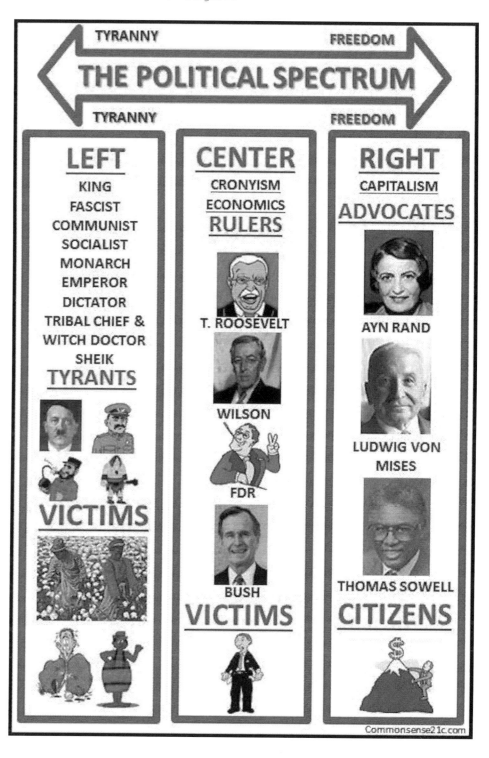

THE EXTREME LEFT OF THE POLITICAL SPECTRUM-A DICTATORSHIP:

The ultimate objective of the Aristocracy is to obtain dictatorial powers!

The Dictatorship, complete control by the Aristocracy, goes by many names. Communism, Socialism, Dictator, Fascism, Monarchy, Emperor, Sheik and Tribal Chief - witch Doctor are examples of the extreme left of the political spectrum. Oppression of the individual is the defining principle of a Dictatorship, The title of the Despot and the justification for the coercion are the only difference between these forms of Tyranny. Unlimited coercion of the individual is the hallmark of all the forms of Tyranny and all occupy the extreme left of the political spectrum.

The center of the political spectrum-"Cronyism Economics":
The Aristocracy has achieved partial control of the economy and Cronyism economics is our current Economic System. However, some individual rights have survived. With varying degrees of control, the government makes some economic decisions for the individual, controls some of the actions of both individuals and businesses by issuance of licenses. The Aristocracy obtains economic advantages by issuing laws, rules and regulations that control economic activities. These same rules can be used to punish the political opposition and extort support for the Aristocracy's agenda.

Innovation that reduces the production cost and creates new products also creates a class of technologically challenged producers whose products are obsolete. These technologically challenged producers are frequently members of the Aristocracy and often enact rules to maintain the status quo, quashing their technologically advantaged competitors. Of course the higher costs are passed on to the consumer, thus eliminating the advantages of innovation (sometimes called the technology dividend). Growth of Cronyism Economic Policies ensures a declining economy and eventual degeneration into a Dictatorship.

The extreme right, Capitalism: The government protects the individual's rights. Pure Capitalism, like the temperature, absolute zero in physics has never been achieved and is simply a theory. History shows that prosperity and general wellbeing increase with individual freedom and decline with coercion.

DICTATORSHIP — THE EXTREME LEFT:

The first of three cartoons that define a Dictatorship.

20st CENTURY DICTATORS AND THE ARISTOCRACY'S 21st CENTURY DECLARATION:

DICTATOR-THE EXTREME LEFT
(COMMUNISM, SOCIALISM, MONARCHY, DICTATOR, EMPEROR, SHEIK, TRIBAL CHIEF-WITCH DOCTOR etc.)

20th CENTURY DICTATORS

| HITLER | MUSSOLINI | STALIN | CASTRO |

DEFINING CHARACTERISTIC:
UNLIMITED COERCION OF THE INDIVIDUAL
RESULTS:
THE PEOPLE: POVERTY, DESPAIR, WAR, PERSECUTION FOR POLITICAL DISSENT (CAPITAL OFFENSE)
THE ARISTOCRACY: REIGNED WITH UNLIMITED POWER & WEALTH

21st CENTURY DICTATOR?

 THE ARISTOCRACY DECLARED A DICTATORSHIP ON 2/24/2011 BY STATING THAT ONLY LAWS APPROVED BY THE ARISTOCRACY WOULD BE ENFORCED. SINCE THAT DECLARATION, EXECUTIVE ORDERS HAVE BEEN ENFORCED AS THE LAW OF THE LAND.

DUE TO INEFFECTIVE OPPOSITION TO THIS DECLARATION THE ARISTOCRACY IS CONSOLIDATING ITS POWER

Commonsense21c.com

The second of three cartoons that defines the Economic characteristics of a Dictatorship.

ARISTOCRACY'S ECONOMY-1
A DEFINITION OF THE FAR LEFT-A DICTATORSHIP

21st CENTURY SERF:
SLAVES FROM DAWN TO DUSK
PRODUCING THE
ARISTOCRACY'S WEALTH

POLITICAL DISSENT:
WILL NOT BE TOLERATED!
A CAPITAL OFFENSE IN A DICTATORSHIP!

ENTREPRENEUR:
INNOVATION IS PUNISHED BY CONFISCATION
OF WEALTH, IMPRISONMENT OR EVEN DEATH.
IF SUPPRESSION OF THE INNOVATION IS
IMPRACTICAL, THE ARISTOCRACY CLAIMS THE
CREDIT AND VILIFIES THE ENTREPRENEUR

CITIZENS DISARMED:
ARMED RESISTANCE TO OPPRESSION IS
IMPOSSIBLE!
RESISTANCE IS FUTILE

Commonsense21c.com

This cartoon defines the economic characteristics of a dictatorship.

ARISTOCRACY'S ECONOMY-2
A DEFINITION OF THE FAR LEFT-A DICTATORSHIP

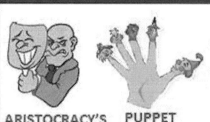

ARISTOCRACY'S PRESS SEC. **PUPPET PRESS**

PUPPET PRESS:
1. PRAISES THE ARISTOCRACY'S SUCCESS & PLANS
2. FLOODS MEDIA WITH THE IRRELEVANT TO AVOID DISCUSSION OF REAL ISSUES
3. VILIFIES THE ARISTOCRACY'S ENEMIES

BUREAUCRACY:
ENHANCES THE POWER & WEALTH OF THE ARISTOCRACY BY MAKING ECONOMIC DECISIONS FOR THE INDIVIDUAL & ENFORCING THOSE DECISIONS.

ARISTOCRACY:
1. CONTROLS ALL THE WEALTH PRODUCED BY THE 21st CENTURY SERF
2. MAKES UNLIMITED RULES AND REGULATIONS GOVERNING THE ECONOMY TO MAINTAIN ABSOLUTE CONTROL OF THE INDIVIDUAL
3. ATTACKS ANY ACT OF INSURRECTION WITH DEADLY FORCE
4. LIVES IN ABSOLUTE LUXURY WHILE THE 21st CENTURY SERF EXIST IN POVERTY & DESPAIR

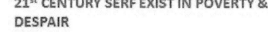

Commonsense21c.com

CRONYISM ECONOMICS-THE CENTER OF THE POLITICAL SPECTRUM:

Quote by Gideon J. Tucker, 1826
"NO MAN'S LIFE, LIBERTY OR PROPERTY ARE SAFE WHILE THE LEGISLATURE IS IN SESSION."

This is the best description of Cronyism Economics ever penned. The Bureaucracy has established a perpetual legislative session.

Cronyism Economics is a mixture of government coercion and individual freedom. It is a fluid condition changing with the balance of power between the Aristocracy and Libertarians. Since the late 1880's, the Aristocracy's wealth and power has enjoyed almost constant growth. Individual freedom has been continually eroded by reinterpretation of the Constitution, aggressive action by the Executive Branch (the President and the Bureaucracy) and Congressional action. The economic decisions made by the Bureaucracy for the individual have slowly increased. These economic decisions enhanced Aristocracy's wealth and power, while eroding individual freedom. Of course the cost of these economic decisions is borne by the consumer. The increased costs caused by Bureaucratic rules erode overall standard of living. The description and consequences of "Cronyism Economics" are contained in the next seven cartoons.

This cartoon focuses on FREEDOM V/S PROSPERITY, EARMARKS, and
MORTGAGES TO POOR CREDIT RISK AND CASH FOR CLUNKERS.

CRONYISM ECONOMICS-1

FREEDOM V/S PROSPERITY

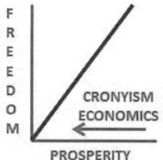

HISTORICAL EVIDENCE PROVES THAT
THE MOST INDIVIDUAL FREEDOMS
WERE ALSO THE MOST PROSPEROUS

CRONYISM
ECONOMICS

FREEDOM

PROSPERITY

EARMARKS

CRONYISM ECONOMICS SYSTEM DEPLOYS
CAPITAL TO ENHANCE THE ARISTOCRACY'S
POWER & WEALTH AT THE TAXPAYER'S EXPENSE

MORTGAGES TO POOR CREDIT RISKS

THE PRACTICE OF MORTGAGING HOMES TO POOR
CREDIT RISKS INVITES FORECLOSURE AND AN
ECONOMIC CRISIS. BOTH CREDITOR & LENDER ARE
VICTIMS.   AN ECONOMIC CRISIS INCREASES
DEPENDENCE ON THE GOVERNMENT – ENHANCING
THE ARISTOCRACY'S POWER

"CASH FOR CLUNKERS"

SALVAGING FUNCTIONING AUTOMOBILES IS
SIMPLY DEPLETING THE NATION'S WEALTH. THE
RESULT WAS INCREASING THE COST OF USED
CARS THAT PROVIDE TRANSPORTATION TO THE
POOR. JUSTIFICATION: THE "GREAT GLOBAL
WARMING SCAM"

Commonsense21c.com

This cartoon describes the effects of Bureaucratic rules on the economy and Internal Revenue Service's (IRS) mission to control and punish political dissent.

CRONYISM ECONOMICS - 2

THE BUREAUCRACY

THE ARISTOCRACY USES THE BUREAUCRACY TO CREATE RULES CONTROLLING THE ECONOMY, THE INDIVIDUAL'S ECONOMIC CHOICES & ACTIONS. THE BUREAUCRACY ENFORCES THESE RULES ON A "GUILTY UNTIL PROVEN INNOCENT " BASIS.

EACH NEW RULE ENHANCES THE ARISTOCRACY'S POWER AND WEALTH AT THE EXPENSE OF THE CONSUMER.

CONGRESS ESCAPES THE BLAME FOR RULES THAT DRAW CRITICISM & GAINS SUPPORT BY DENOUNCING AN OUT OF CONTROL BUREAUCRACY .

EXAMPLE

INCOME TAX

IRS VICTIM

IRS – THE ARISTOCRACY'S CHOICE TO PUNISH POLITICAL DISSENT

1. CREATES HUGE QUANTITIES OF RULES THAT FEW KNOW, CAN UNDERSTAND OR COMPLY WITH
2. ENFORCES THOSE RULES ON A "GUILTY UNTIL PROVEN INNOCENT" BASIS
3. ENFORCEMENT IS GENERALLY CONFISCATION OF VICTIM'S BANK ACCOUNT

Commonsense21c.com

Aristocracy tries to advance its agenda by disarming the Patriots.

CRONYISM ECONOMICS - 3

EXECUTIVE ORDERS

YOUR RIGHTS & WEALTH DISAPPEAR WITH THE *STROKE* OF A PEN

CONGRESS IS IRRELEVANT

CLEARLY UNCONSTITUTIONAL
THE CONSTITUTION
Article. I.
Section. 1.
All legislative Powers herein granted shall be vested in a Congress of the United States, which shall consist of a Senate and House of Representatives.

DISARM PATRIOTS

ARMED PATRIOT PROTECTOR OF THE REPUBLIC

DISARMAMENT OF THE PATRIOT IS THE PRELUDE TO OPPRESSION. HITLER'S 1st PRIORITY WAS TO DISARM THE PUBLIC (ESPECIALLY THE JEWS).

21st CENTURY SERF

THE ARMED CITIZEN OR 21st CENTURY SERF?

THE ARISTOCRACY'S 1st ATTEMPT TO DISARM THE PATRIOT LEXINGTON GREEN

The Aristocracy, the Puppet Press and a Bipartisan Congress advance the Aristocracy's agenda by proclaiming a "living breathing Constitution.

CRONYISM ECONOMICS - 4

A "LIVING BREATHING CONSTITUTION?"

REINTERPRETING THE CONSTITUTION - 5 SUPREME COURT JUDGES REQUIRED

THE UNITED STATES CONSTITUTION IS BOTH DIFFICULT AND TIME CONSUMING TO AMEND. THE ARISTOCRACY HAD TO FIND AN EASIER WAY TO USURP INDIVIDUAL RIGHTS. SIMPLE! JUST REINTERPRET THE TEXT.

THE "PUPPET PRESS"

1. CONTROLLED BY THE ARISTOCRACY.
2. PRAISES THE ARISTOCRACY'S AGENDA.
3. APPLY THE "POLITICS OF PERSONAL DESTRUCTION" TO ENEMIES.
4. FLOOD MEDIA WITH DRIVEL TO PREVENT CRITICISM OF THE ARISTOCRACY.
5. THE ARISTOCRACY'S PROPAGANDA MACHINE.

ADOLPH HITLER:

"BY THE SKILLFUL AND SUSTAINED USE OF PROPAGANDA, ONE CAN MAKE A PEOPLE SEE EVEN HEAVEN AS HELL OR AN EXTREMELY WRETCHED LIFE AS PARADISE."

A BIPARTISAN CONGRESS

THE HOLY GRAIL OF THE PUPPET PRESS! BIPARTISANSHIP REMOVES OPPOSITION TO ARISTOCRACY'S AGENDA. NEW LAWS ARE ENACTED WITHOUT RESTRAINT. WE DON'T NEED ANY MORE STINKING LAWS!

The Aristocracy uses the Great Global Warming Scam, Energy Alchemy, and Maintaining the "Status Quo" to advance its agenda.

CRONYISM ECONOMICS-5

THE GREAT GLOBAL WARMING SCAM
THE ARISTOCRACY'S MOST INGENIOUS SCAM!

TO AVOID A FICTIONAL CATASTROPHE, THE INDIVIDUAL MUST ACCEPT A REDUCED STANDARD OF LIVING AND SURRENDER FREEDOM

OBJECTIVE: INCREASE THE ARISTOCRACY'S POWER & WEALTH

ENERGY ALCHEMY

FOSSIL FUEL IS AND WILL BE THE MOST ECONOMICAL FORM OF ENERGY.

THE ARISTOCRACY USES THE "GREAT GLOBAL WARMING SCAM" AND FEAR OF DEPLETION OF FOSSIL FUEL TO JUSTIFY FUNDING "ENERGY ALCHEMY"

THE FUNDING OF "ENERGY ALCHEMY" INCREASES THE ARISTOCRACY'S WEALTH & POWER.

THE ARISTOCRACY MAINTAINS THE "STATUS QUO"

INNOVATION REDUCES THE COST OF CREATING WEALTH BUT CAN MAKE WHOLE INDUSTRIES OBSOLETE.

THE TECHNICALLY CHALLENGED ARISTOCRACY SUPPRESSES INNOVATION.

1. INNOVATION CREATES WEALTH.
2. THE "STATUS QUO" STIFLES PROGRESS.

Commonsense21c.com

The Aristocracy's Energy Policy, Anti-Trust laws and Victimless Crimes advances its agenda.

CRONYISM ECONOMICS-6

ARISTOCRACY'S ENERGY POLICY!

IN THE 1960'S A MEDIA CAMPAIGN CALLED FOR A COMPREHENSIVE ENERGY POLICY
THE GOVERNMENT BEGAN TO MEDDLE IN OIL PRODUCTION & EXPLORATION

GASOLINE PRICES INCREASED FROM ABOUT $0.35 / GALLON IN THE 1960'S TO ABOUT $3.50 TODAY
THE ARISTOCRACY'S POWER & WEALTH SOARED WITH THE PRICES

ANTI-TRUST LAWS

GUILTY

VAGUE, NON-OBJECTIVE LAWS WITH THE ILLEGALITY OF SOME OFFENSES DEPENDENT ON THE "INTENT" OF THE ACCUSED

BOTH PROSECUTION AND GUILT ARE MORE DEPENDENT ON POLITICAL INFLUENCE & PRE-TRIAL PUBLICITY THAN THE ALLEGED MISCONDUCT

VICTIMLESS CRIMES

1. JUSTIFIED BY THE MORALITY OF THE ARISTOCRACY
2. VIOLATIONS RESULTING IN INCARCERATION OF THE OFFENDER
3. THE ECONOMIC COST TO BOTH THE VIOLATOR AND SOCIETY IS HUGE

THE ACTUAL REASON FOR VICTIMLESS CRIMES IS ECONOMIC
IN A CALIFORNIA REFERENDUM ON MARIJUANA, THE ALCOHOL INDUSTRY FINANCED THE OPPOSITION. LEGAL MARIJUANA WOULD REDUCE DEMAND FOR ALCOHOL BEVERAGES.

Commonsense21c.com

Inflationary policies are always a part of Cronyism Economics and are a major cause of economic crisis.

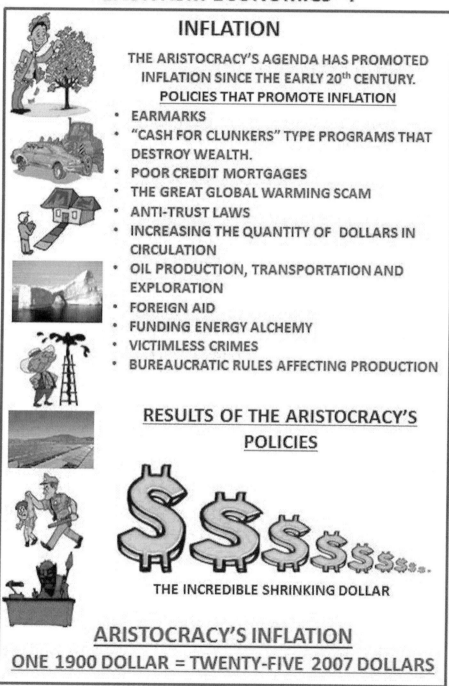

THE EXTREME RIGHT OF THE POLITICAL SPECTRUM-CAPITALISM:

A reporter asked Ayn Rand if she were a conservative. Her answer "there is nothing left to conserve, I am a radical for Capitalism."

The Encarta Dictionary defines Capitalism as "an economic system based on the private ownership of the means of production and distribution of goods, characterized by a free competitive market and motivation by profit."

Pure Capitalism "the unknown ideal" has never actually existed. Like the temperature "absolute zero" and the speed of light, Capitalism has only been approached. Because pure Capitalism has never existed, cartoons displaying the results of Capitalism are not possible as was done with the Dictatorship Economic System or the Cronyism Economic System.

When the United States Constitution was adopted the economic system created was as close to Capitalism as has ever existed. This "Near Capitalist System" continued through the 19th century and early 20th century. The "Near Capitalist System" generated a period of technological achievement and converted the United States from a "40 acres and a mule" economy into an economic powerhouse. The next four cartoons describe the achievements obtained in a "Near Capitalist Economy." Great achievements are obtained when the Entrepreneur is free from the Aristocracy's intervention.

The following four cartoons show the triumph of even a "Near Capitalist System.

CAPITALISM-THE UNKNOWN IDEAL:

"CAPITALISM, THE UNKNOWN IDEAL" is the first of four cartoons used to define the "Capitalism Economic System" and describe the achievements that are achieved when the "Cronyism Economic System" approaches the freedom of the "Capitalist Economic System."

CAPITALISM – THE UNKNOWN IDEAL

THE GOVERNMENT

THE GOVERNMENT ACTIVELY PROTECTS INDIVIDUAL RIGHTS

THE ENTREPRENEUR

THE ENTREPRENEUR USES INNOVATION, CAPITAL AND HARD WORK TO CREATE WEALTH & PROFIT

ALL SOCIETY BENEFITS WHEN INNOVATION RESULTS IN NEW PRODUCTS & REDUCED PRODUCTION COST

THE ECONOMY

THE NATION'S WEALTH EXPANDS DRIVEN BY UNRESTRICTED INNOVATION AND ENHANCES THE STANDARD OF LIVING

THE INDIVIDUAL

- **THE INDIVIDUAL MAKES ALL ECONOMIC DECISIONS**
- **INNOVATION (NEW PRODUCTS AND MORE EFFICIENT PRODUCTION) ENHANCES THE VALUE OF THE INDIVIDUAL'S PRODUCTIVITY**

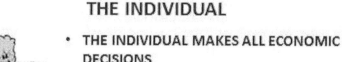

Commonsense21c.com

ACHIEVEMENTS OF A "NEAR CAPITALIST SYSTEM"-1:

The cartoon, "CAPITALIST SYSTEM"-1, describes the accomplishments of an economic system that approaches the Capitalist System.

- Capitalism applied to agriculture.
- Mr. Rockefeller was vilified as a "Robber Baron" because his innovations netted him a vast fortune and removed the technologically challenged competitors from the marketplace.

ACHIEVEMENTS OF A "NEAR CAPITALIST SYSTEM"-1

AGRICULTURE

AN INCREDIBLE TRANSFORMATION

THE PRODUCTIVITY OF THE FARMER SOARED WITH THE ADVENT OF FARM EQUIPMENT. "40 ACRES & A MULE" WAS REPLACED BY "1000 ACRES AND A TRACTOR"

THE PORTION OF THE POPULATION REQUIRED TO PRODUCE FOOD WAS REDUCED FROM 41% TO 1.9% RELEASING A TREMENDOUS AMOUNT OF MAN-POWER FOR PRODUCTION OF NEW PRODUCTS

ENERGY, MR. ROCKEFELLER'S INNOVATION

COTTAGE INDUSTRY

MR. ROCKEFELLER'S INNOVATIONS REDUCED THE PRICE OF KEROSENE FROM $0.58 TO $0.074 PER GALLON

OIL REFINERY

ENERGY IS SOURCE OF PROGRESS

PROGRESS IS ACCOMPLISHED BY REPLACING OR SUPPLEMENTING MUSCLES WITH MECHANICAL ENERGY

Commonsense21c.com

More examples of the achievement of the "Near Capitalist System:
- Aluminum Industry
- Electric Utility Industry

ACHIEVEMENTS OF A "NEAR CAPITALIST SYSTEM"-2

ALUMINUM INDUSTRY

CHARLES MARTIN HALL, THE FOUNDER OF ALCOA, CONVERTED ALUMINUM FROM AN EXPENSIVE LABORATORY CURIOSITY TO A COMMON CONSTRUCTION MATERIAL WITH UNIQUE PROPERTIES.

ALUMINUM 'S UNIQUE PROPERTIES MADE INVENTIONS FEASIBLE AND REDUCED THE COST WHILE INCREASING THE PERFORMANCE OF CURRENT PRODUCTS

ELECTRIC UTILITY INDUSTRY

THOMAS EDISON DEVELOPED THE LIGHT BLUB AND CREATED THE ELECTRICAL UTILITY INDUSTRY

Commonsense21c.com

The early, very successful Entrepreneurs were often termed "Robber Barons" by the Puppet Press. Who were the real "Robber Barons"? Was it the Entrepreneurs, who created the wealth, or the politicians who attempted to grant economic favors to their supporters that were the real Robber Barons?

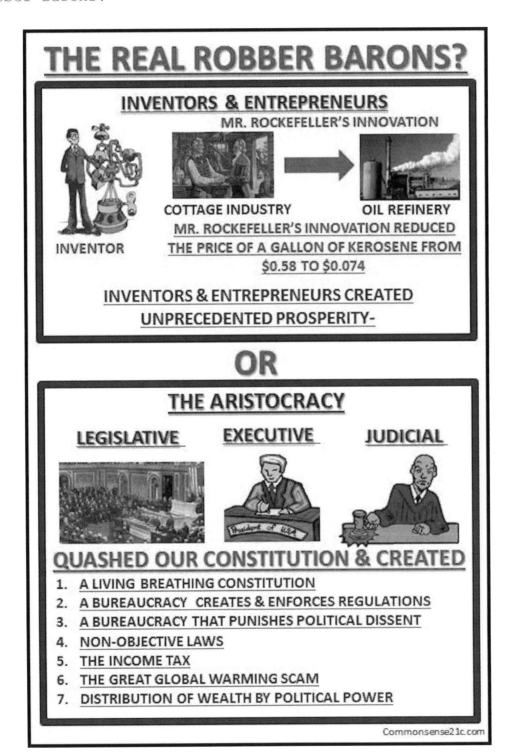

THE ARISTOCRACY'S AGENDA-I:

The United States Constitution established an economic system as close to Capitalism as had ever existed. The Aristocracy's control of both the economy and the individual had been destroyed by the American Revolution. This cartoon focuses on the Aristocracy's agenda to regain their power and wealth.

The second cartoon completes the description of the Aristocracy's Agenda to regain its power and wealth.

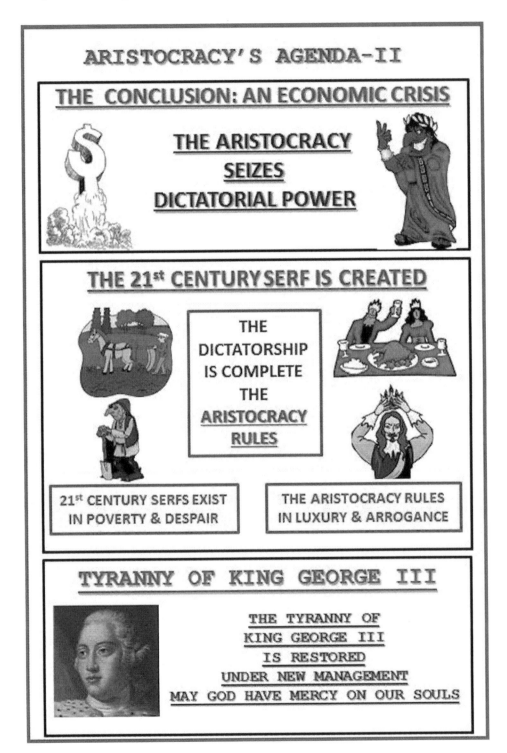

THE BUREAUCRACY-THE ARISTOCRACY'S WEAPON OF CHOICE:

The Bureaucracy was established by the Congress to escape the blame for controversial legislation.

Special interest groups routinely petition the Congress to pass laws that give them an economic advantage. Congress wants to placate these powerful constituents, but if two special interest groups have opposing interests, legislation to satisfy both groups may not be possible.

Congress's solution was to create a Bureaucracy instructed to craft "fair and just" rules that provide a resolution to the conflict. Who could argue with a "fair and just" solution? The Congress is credited for solving a difficult problem. If Bureaucracy's "fair and just" rules are unpopular, Congress claims that it is the result of "out-of- control" Bureaucracy and gains more approval by promising to "reign in" and punish the "out-of-control" Bureaucracy. Is there another kind of Bureaucracy?

The first bureaucracy, Interstate Commerce Commission (ICC) was born in 1888 to resolve the conflict between the Grange (a powerful farm lobby) and the railroads. The ICC rules were ineffective due to delays caused by litigation. So, a few years later, the Congress made the ICC's rules and rulings effective until overturned by the Courts. This change made the Bureaucracy's victim "guilty until proven innocent in a court of law." Few victims have the resources to challenge the Bureaucracy in court and even a prosperous victim can be bankrupted by the litigation.

For over 100 years, the ICC (now defunct) regulations increased the cost of transportation, passing this cost on to the consumer. The ICC regulations made it so difficult for the railroads to function that the government was forced to seize the railroads to provide adequate transportation for the war effort during World War I. For the details, see the book, "21st CENTURY COMMON SENSE", Chapter 8-THE BUREAUCRACY – ICC.

All bureaucratic rules increase the Aristocracy's wealth and power. The Aristocracy wins and the people pay the bill.

The following 18 cartoons highlight the birth of the Bureaucracy, rules created by the Bureaucracy, and the effects of these rules on the economy.

BUREAUCRACY-101 is a basic criticism of the Bureaucracy.

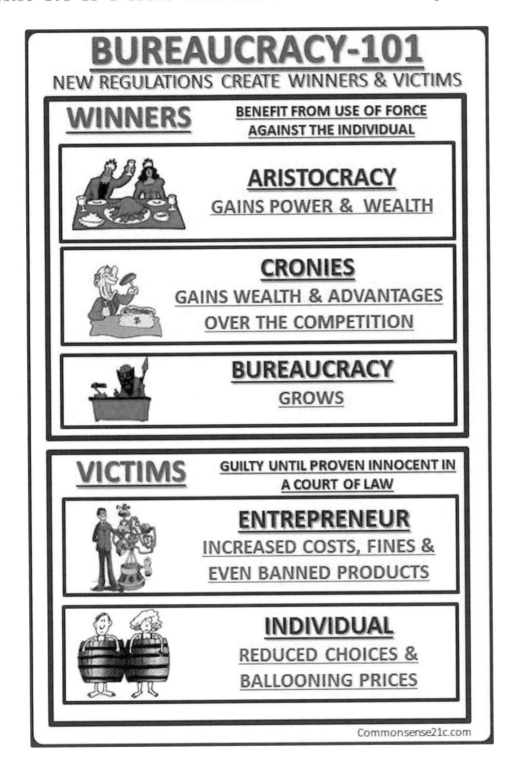

This cartoon focuses on the birth of the Bureaucracy.

BIRTH OF THE BUREAUCRACY-1888

RAILROADS & THE GRANGE (A LARGE FARMERS ORGANIZATION) SEEK FAVORABLE FREIGHT RATES BY APPLYING PRESSURE TO THE CONGRESS

THE GRANGE WANTED LOW RATES

THE RAILROADS WANTED HIGH RATES

BOTH WANTED ADVANTAGES OVER THEIR ADVERSARY PROVIDED BY GOVERNMENT FORCE

ATTEMPTING TO PLACATE BOTH SIDES, CONGRESS CREATES THE INTERSTATE COMMERCE COMMISSION-

THE BUREAUCRACY IS BORN!

THE BUREAUCRACY IS GIVEN THE POWER TO CREATE & ENFORCE RULES ON A "GUILTY UNTIL PROVEN INNOCENT IN A COURT OF LAW" BASIS

THE BUREAUCRACY

THE ARISTOCRACY'S WEAPON OF CHOICE TO REWARD THEIR CRONIES AND PUNISH POLITICAL DISSENT!

Commonsense21c.com

BUREAUCRATIC POWERS:

This cartoon lists the Bureaucracy's awesome powers. The Aristocracy found that the rulings of the Bureaucracy were not effective due to delays caused by litigation. Congress solved this problem by making the Bureaucratic rules and sanctions legally binding until overturned by the Courts. Of course, this made the victim "guilty until proven innocent in a Court of Law. Resistance is futile?

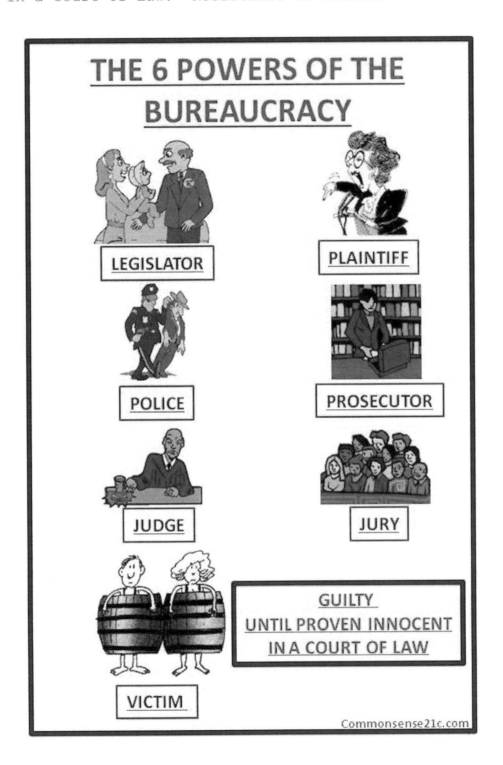

ENFORCERS OF TYRANNY:

This cartoon compares "enforcers of tyranny"-today and in 1776.

THE ARISTOCRACY'S WEAPON OF CHOICE:

This cartoon labels the Bureaucracy the Aristocracy's "weapon of choice" and explains why.

THE BUREAUCRACY-
THE ARISTOCRACY'S WEAPON OF CHOICE

THE ARISTOCRACY'S OBJECTIVE:
1. INCREASE THE ARISTOCRACY'S POWER
2. REWARD POLITICAL SUPPORT
3. PUNISH POLITICAL DISSENT

THE BUREAUCRACY
1. CREATES RULES
2. ENFORCES RULES ON A
"A GUILTY UNTIL PROVEN INNOCENT IN A COURT OF LAW" BASIS
SEIZING THE VICTIM'S WEALTH

VICTIM!
SOURCE OF WEALTH
USED TO ACHIEVE THE ARISTOCRACY'S OBJECTIVE

CONFISCATION OF YOUR WEALTH IS ONLY A PEN STROKE AWAY!

IS RESISTANCE FUTILE?

Commonsense21c.com

Cartoon presents the Aristocracy's mandate to the Bureaucracy and the consequences of implementing that mandate.

THE BUREAUCRACY'S MANDATE

- CREATE RULES THAT CONTROL THE ECONOMY BENEFITING THE ARISTOCRACY
- ENFORCE THOSE RULES WITH UNRESTRICTED FORCE

RESULTS

THE ARISTOCRACY'S
POWER & WEALTH INCREASES WITH EVERY NEW REGULATION

THE 21st CENTURY SERF

EXISTS IN POVERTY & DESPAIR

A DICTATORSHIP

EACH NEW RULE MOVES THE ECONOMY TO THE FURTHER TO LEFT

A DICTATORSHIP IS INEVITABLE

Commonsense21c.com

NEW REGULATIONS:

Why does the Aristocracy direct the Bureaucracy to create new rules? The Aristocracy cannot control a nation of law abiding citizens but a nation of criminals is controlled automatically. A large volume of ambiguous, unsung rules enforced on a "guilty until proven innocent" creates a nation of criminals, providing the Aristocracy with the power it craves.

BUREAUCRACY'S REGULATIONS:

This cartoon also discusses new Bureaucratic rules and the economic consequences.

BUREAUCRACY'S REGULATIONS

THE PURPOSE (AS ADVERTISED)

1. ENHANCE THE INDIVIDUAL'S LIFE
2. PREVENT THE INDIVIDUAL FROM MAKING HARMFUL DECISIONS
3. PROTECT THE ENVIRONMENT

BUREAUCRAT

RESULTS

THE ARISTOCRACY

INCREASE THE POWER & WEALTH

INDIVIDUAL

1. INFLATION (INCREASED COST OF LIVING)
2. FREEDOM OF CHOICE LIMITED

ENTREPRENEUR-INVENTOR

1. INCREASE COST
2. LIMITED PRODUCT FEATURES
3. INVENTIONS BANNED

BUREAUCRAT

1. INCREASED BUDGET
2. INCREASED POWER

Commonsense21c.com

The Aristocracy uses the Bureaucracy to destroy the effectiveness of its enemies.

ARISTOCRACY'S TACTIC TO "TAKE OUT" THE OPPOSITION

CONVERT THE OPPOSITION INTO CRIMINALS

HOW?
ENACT COMPLICATED, AMBIGUOUS REGULATIONS, WITH WHICH THE OPPOSITION IS IGNORANT OF OR UNABLE TO COMPLY.
EXAMPLE: IRS REGULATIONS

OPPOSITION IS VILIFIED BY THE PUPPET PRESS & PROSECUTED FOR THE VIOLATION

USE OF THE BUREAUCRACY MAKES THE VICTIM "GUILTY UNTIL PROVEN INNOCENT"

BANKRUPTCY OR INCARCERATION "TAKES OUT" THE OPPOSITION

Commonsense21c.com

THE ARISTOCRACY SELECTS THE VICTIM-BUREAUCRACY:

The Aristocracy selects the Bureaucracy's victim. Once the victim is selected, vilification by the Puppet Press precedes the Bureaucracy's guilty verdict. Win or lose, challenging the Bureaucracy in Court may bankrupt the victim. If the Bureaucracy loses in Court it can always change the rules and try again.

THE ARISTOCRACY SELECTS THE VICTIM

VICTIM SELECTION CRITERIA

- POLITICAL OPPOSITION
- ECONOMIC THREAT TO A CRONY
- PUBLISHES UNFRIENDLY NEWS
- SUPPORTS POLITICAL OPPOSITION
- FAILS TO SUPPORT THE ARISTOCRACY'S AGENDA

THE BUREAUCRACY ACTS

BUREAUCRAT

ENTREPRENEUR
(VICTIM)

THE PROSECUTION

VICTIM

- THE PUPPET PRESS VILIFIES THE VICTIM
- VICTIM IS GUILTY UNTIL PROVEN INNOCENT IN A COURT OF LAW
- THE COST OF CONTESTING THE BUREAUCRACY ACTION IN COURT COULD BANKRUPT THE VICTIM, WIN OR LOSE
- IF THE VICTIM WINS, THE BUREAUCRACY CAN CREATE NEW RULES WITH NEW VIOLATIONS.

SELECTIVE ENFORCEMENT OF IRS RULES:

The eleventh Bureaucracy cartoon highlights the selective enforcement of IRS rules to harass the Aristocracy's enemies and benefit the Aristocracy's cronies.

SELECTIVE ENFORCEMENT OF IRS RULES

ARISTOCRACY SELECTS THE VICTIM
IRS NEUTRALIZES THE VICTIM
PROSECUTION:
- VICTIM VILIFIED BY THE PUPPET PRESS
- ELIMINATES POLITICAL OPPOSITION
- CONTROLS THE PUPPET PRESS
- PUNISHES POLITICAL DISSENT
- COERCES SUPPORT FOR THE ARISTOCRACY'S AGENDA
- ELIMINATES CRONIES' COMPETITORS

SELECTIVE ENFORCEMENT REWARDS THE ARISTOCRACY'S CRONIES

IRS PUNISHES THE ARISTOCRACY'S ENEMIES

IRS

VICTIM

IRS REWARDS THE ARISTOCRACY'S CRONIES

TAXES? WHAT TAXES?
ONLY THE LITTLE PEOPLE PAY TAXES

THE BUREAUCRACY & THE "STATUS QUO":

One purpose of the Bureaucracy is to maintain the "Status Quo." Innovation creates new products rendering current products obsolete or reducing the cost. A prosperous industrialist's market can be eliminated by a superior product or by a competitor's improved process with lower cost or better quality.

The prosperous industrialists are frequently members of the Aristocracy and use the Bureaucracy to suppress the competition that threatens their market.

When innovation is suppressed, the consumer pays with increased cost and loses the utility of new products.

THE BUREAUCRACY & THE "STATUS QUO:"

THE ENTREPRENEUR'S INNOVATION

MY WHEEL WILL CREATE TREMENDOUS WEALTH

ENTREPRENEUR

THE BUREAUCRAT'S DECISION

ABSOLUTELY NOT!
THE WHEEL IS PROHIBITED

- THE WHEEL WOULD DAMAGE THE TRAILS-THE ENVIRONMENT MUST BE PROTECTED
- THE PORTERS' UNION WOULD BE DESTROYED. THE PORTER JOB WOULD BE ELIMINATED
- SKILLED WORKERS' JOBS MUST BE PROTECTED

BUREAUCRAT

THE REWARDS OF INNOVATION

PROMETHEUS PRESENTS THE GIFT OF FIRE TO MANKIND

THE GODS PUNISH PROMETHEUS FOR PRESENTING FIRE TO MANKIND PUNISHMENT FOR INNOVATION IS NOW THE FUNCTION OF THE BUREAUCRACY

Commonsense21c.com

BUREAUCRACY'S VICTIM:

The Bureaucracy squeezes its victim.

It is David (the victim) and Goliath (the Bureaucracy), all over again but with different results.

The Aristocrat's dilemma and the Bureaucracy in action.

THE ARISTOCRACY'S DILEMMA

ARISTOCRACY

BUREAUCRACY

TWO POWERFUL CRONIES WERE DEMANDING CONFLICTING ECONOMIC FAVORS. THE CONGRESS WAS UNABLE TO FIND A SUITABLE COMPROMISE AND WAS CONCERNED ABOUT REPERCUSSIONS DURING THE NEXT ELECTION. SO THE CONGRESS CREATED THE BUREAUCRACY WITH THE INSTRUCTIONS TO PRODUCE A "REASONABLE AND JUST" COMPROMISE TO SETTLE THE ISSUE. DELAYS BY COURT CHALLENGES TO THE BUREAUCRACY'S RULINGS MADE THE BUREAUCRACY INEFFECTIVE.

CONGRESS MADE THE BUREAUCRACY'S RULES AND DECISIONS LAWFUL UNTIL OVERTURNED BY THE COURTS, THUS ESTABLISHING THE AWESOME POWER OF THE BUREAUCRACY. TO UNDERSTAND THE BUREAUCRACY'S POWER AND MANDATE, READ "A TOBY'S FABLE: EGGS, INC. THE FARMER AND THE BUREAUCRACY" - AVAILABLE ON AMAZON.COM

THE BUREAUCRACY

THE ARISTOCRACY'S ENEMY

THE INDEPENDENT SPECIAL PROSECUTOR:

This cartoon focuses on the need for an Independent Special Prosecutor to end the oppression of the Aristocracy's enemies.

INDEPENDENT SPECIAL PROSECUTOR V/S THE BUREAUCRACY

INDEPENDENT PROSECUTOR WITH THE POWER TO

1. IDENTIFY & HALT THE OPPRESSION OF POLITICAL DISSENT BY THE BUREAUCRACY & JUSTICE DEPARTMENT

2. PROSECUTE THOSE RESPONSIBLE FOR THE OPPRESSION

A REPUBLIC CANNOT SURVIVE THE BUREAUCRATIC OPPRESSION OF THE ARISTOCRACY'S ENEMIES AND ECONOMIC FAVORS TO THE ARISTOCRACY'S CRONIES

A SPECIAL PROSECUTOR MAY BE OUR ONLY CHANCE TO AVOID A BLOODY REVOLUTION & NO ONE WANTS TO REPEAT LEXINGTON GREEN

POLITICAL DISSENT: THE LIFE BLOOD OF THE REPUBLIC

Commonsense21c.com

THE BUNDY RANCH V/S ARISTOCRACY:

The Aristocracy used the Bureaucracy to victimize the Bundy Ranch in the pursuit of wealth and power.

BUNDY RANCH V/S ARISTOCRACY
THE ARISTOCRACY'S WEAPON-THE BUREAUCRACY

THE ARISTOCRACY'S OBJECTIVE:
1. INCREASE THE ARISTOCRACY'S POWER & WEALTH
2. REWARD POLITICAL SUPPORT
3. PUNISH POLITICAL DISSENT

THE VICTIM:
PROVIDES THE WEALTH FOR THE BENEFIT OF THE ARISTOCRACY

THE BUREAUCRACY
1. CREATES REGULATIONS
2. ENFORCES REGULATIONS BY CONFISCATING VICTIM'S WEALTH ON "A GUILTY UNTIL PROVEN INNOCENT IN A COURT OF LAW" BASIS.

VICTIM'S DILEMMA !
FEW VICTIMS HAVE THE RESOURCES TO CHALLENGE THE BUREAUCRACY IN COURT

THE CHOICE:
BANKRUPTCY OR SURRENDER?

Commonsense21c.com

Wealth must be produced before it can be consumed or redistributed.

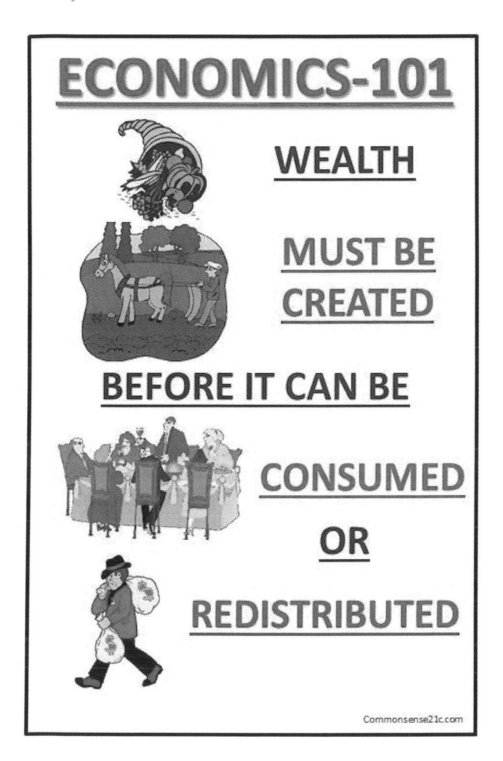

If the Republic is to survive the Bureaucracy must be abolished.

Society's real problem is the creation of wealth.

The relationship that exists between Society and wealth.

THE ECONOMICS OF WEALTH

- WEALTH IS THE GOODS AND SERVICES REQUIRED TO MAINTAIN OUR CIVILIZED SOCIETY
- WEALTH MUST BE PRODUCED BEFORE IT CAN BE CONSUMED OR REDISTRIBUTED

THE WEALTH AVAILABLE TO SOCIETY

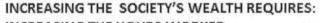

INCREASING THE SOCIETY'S WEALTH REQUIRES:
- INCREASING THE HOURS WORKED
- INNOVATION:
  - MORE EFFICIENT METHODS & BETTER SKILLED WORKERS
  - PRODUCTS EASIER TO PRODUCE
  - PRODUCTS WITH BETTER PERFORMANCE
  - PRODUCTS THAT ELIMINATE THE NEED FOR OTHER PRODUCTS

FORCE AND WEALTH

- THE ARISTOCRACY USES FORCE TO INCREASE ITS WEALTH & POWER
- FORCE CANNOT INCREASE SOCIETY'S WEALTH
- FORCE REDUCES THE <u>INCENTIVE</u> TO PRODUCE WEALTH
- FORCE DESTROYS THE <u>CAPACITY</u> TO PRODUCE WEALTH
- <u>THE SLAVE RARELY PRODUCES MORE THAN THE VALUE OF THE MASTER'S WHIP</u>

<u>SOCIETY'S PROSPERITY REQUIRES FREEDOM & INNOVATION</u>
THE ARISTOCRACY'S WEALTH & POWER IS ACQUIRED BY FORCE AND THAT FORCE CREATES A SOCIETY PLAGUED BY POVERTY & DESPAIR

Commonsense21c.com

ECONOMICS OF TWO ECONOMIC SYSTEMS:

The cartoon shows the difference between Capitalism and Cronyism Economics.

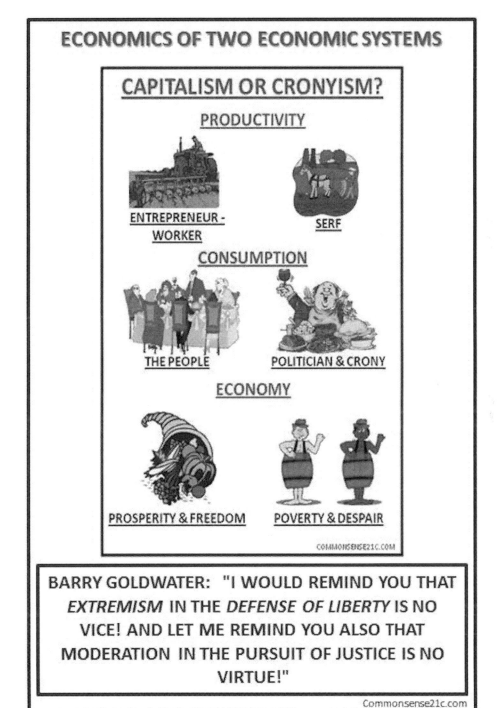

AN ECONOMIC CRISIS CAN DESTROY THE REPUBLIC:

This cartoon explains that an economic crisis is required to convert a Republic into a Dictatorship. Is the Aristocracy's objective to create that economic crisis?

AN ECONOMIC CRISIS CAN DESTROY THE REPUBLIC

THE ARISTOCRACY

HAS DECREED UNCONSTITUTIONAL "EXECUTIVE ORDERS" & APPLIED INFLATIONARY POLICIES THAT UNDERMINE THE ECONOMY.

IS THE ARISTOCRACY'S OBJECTIVE AN ECONOMIC CRISIS?

ENTREPRENEUR (PRODUCER)

INFLATION, EXECUTIVE ORDERS & REGULATIONS SQUEEZE THE PRODUCERS & ELIMINATE JOBS.

ULTIMATE RESULTS: AN ECONOMIC CRISIS!

WHY WOULD THE ARISTOCRACY WANT AN ECONOMIC CRISIS? HITLER & MUSSOLINI USURPED POWER DURING AN ECONOMIC CRISIS

Commonsense21c.com

Inflation is a major contributor to the cause an economic crisis.

INFLATION-STEALTH TAXATION
A TAX ON YOUR WALLET & BANK ACCOUNT
CAUSES OF INFLATION

THE FEDERAL RESERVE AND TREASURY INCREASE CREDIT (DOLLARS) IN CIRCULATION (DEFICIT SPENDING) WITHOUT AN INCREASE IN THE NATION'S WEALTH

ANTI-TRUST LAWS INHIBIT THE INNOVATION AND USE OF THE "ECONOMIES OF SCALE"

BUREAUCRATIC RULES AND REGULATIONS INCREASE THE COST OF PRODUCTION, INHIBIT INNOVATION AND THE USE OF THE "ECONOMIES OF SCALE"

INFLATION IS A MAJOR CAUSE OF ECONOMIC CRISIS

Commonsense21c.com

WHICH IS THE BEST USE OF CAPITAL?

This cartoon asks: "Which is the better use of capital, the entrepreneur's innovation or the Aristocracy's wealth & power?"

The cartoon explains how the Aristocracy policies move the nation toward an economic crisis.

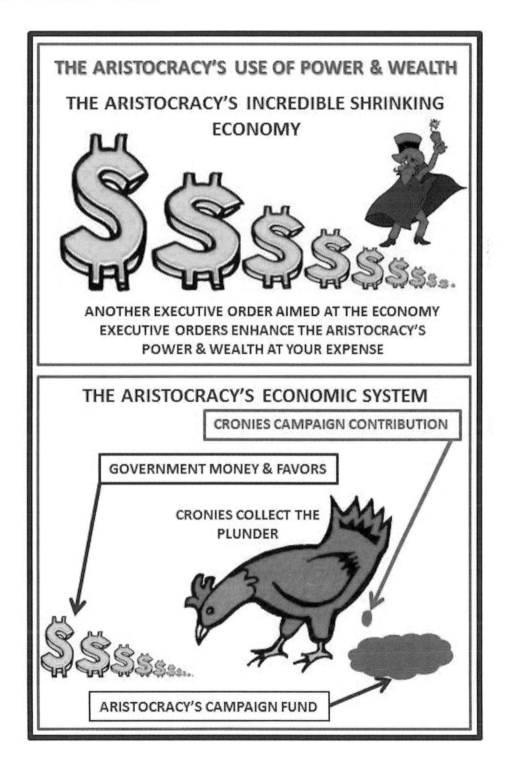

AN ECONOMIC CRISIS DEFINED:

This cartoon answers the question, exactly what is an economic crisis.

AN ECONOMIC CRISIS DEFINED

 MANY BUSINESSES CLOSED & BANKRUPT

- PEOPLE ARE JOBLESS & DEPENDENT ON THE GOVERNMENT FOR FOOD & SHELTER
- MANY USE FORCE TO SURVIVE

 STREETS & PARKS FILLED WITH THE HOMELESS & INDIGENT

- VALUE OF MONEY CHANGES RAPIDLY
- BANKS FAIL
- BARTER REPLACES MONEY AS A MEDIUM OF EXCHANGE

 PRODUCTION FALLS BELOW THE LEVEL REQUIRED TO SUSTAIN SOCIETY

DESPERATION SPAWNS A DICTATORSHIP

ECONOMIC CRISIS BROUGHT HITLER & MUSSOLINI TO POWER

Commonsense21c.com

HOW TO CAUSE AN ECONOMIC CRISIS:

This cartoon displays the actions the Aristocracy is taking to cause an economic crisis.

HOW TO CAUSE AN ECONOMIC CRISIS

INFLATION

INCREASE THE CASH & CREDIT IN CIRCULATION

DEPLETE THE NATION'S WEALTH
INSTITUTE PROGRAMS THAT CONSUME WEALTH

| ENERGY ALCHEMY | PROGRAMS LIKE "CASH FOR CLUNKERS" THAT DESTROY WEALTH | PROTECT THE INEFFICIENT PRODUCER |

DISCOURAGE INNOVATION

BUREAUCRATIC OBSTACLES:
- RULES INCREASE THE COST OF CREATING NEW PRODUCTS
- LICENSES, ENFORCED SPECIFICATIONS & BUREAUCRATIC APPROVAL

BUREAUCRATIC RULES:

- MANDATE EXPENSIVE PROCESSES
- MANDATE COSTLY EMPLOYEE RULES & BENEFITS
- INSPECTIONS & FINES FOR VIOLATING RULES
- ENFORCEMENT FAVORING THE ARISTOCRACY'S CRONIES

REDUCTION OF THE NATION'S WEALTH, INCREASES IN CASH IN CIRCULATION & INCREASES IN THE ARISTOCRACY'S POWER ARE THE MAJOR CAUSE OF AN ECONOMIC CRISIS

Commonsense21c.com

This cartoon evaluates the Aristocracy's claim of economic recovery and comments on who is to blame for our sad economic conditions.

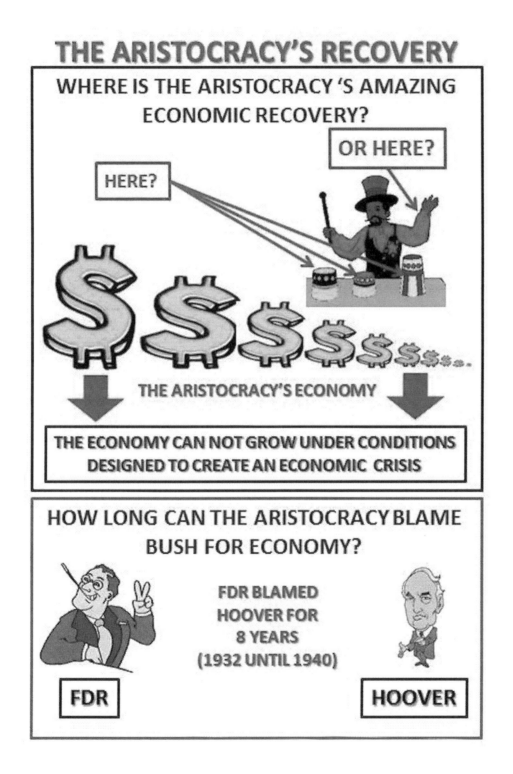

THE CHARACTERISTICS OF ECONOMIC SUCCESS:

This cartoon explains how the characteristics required for success vary between the Capitalist Economic System and the Cronyism Economic System.

THE CHARACTERISTIC OF ECONOMIC SUCCESS

CAPITALISM REQUIRES
INNOVATION

- **PRODUCTS WITH BEST PERFORMANCE, LOWEST COST & HIGHEST QUALITY**
- **PRODUCTS THAT PROVIDE NEW FUNCTIONS & CAPABILITY**
- **ASSURES WEALTH & PROFIT**

RESULTS
- **INCREASES NATION'S WEALTH**
- **ADVANCED TECHNOLOGY ENHANCES THE QUALITY OF LIFE**
- **REDUCES THE REAL COST OF LIVING**
- **PROSPERITY**

CRONYISM ECONOMICS REQUIRES
INFLUENCE

- **COMPETITORS QUASHED**
- **SPECIFICATIONS MANDATE PRODUCT FEATURES & PERFORMANCE**
- **LICENSES RESTRICT ENTRY INTO PROFESSIONS & BUSINESSES**
- **MANDATES CONSUMER PURCHASES**
- **CONSUMER DECISIONS LIMITED OR MADE BY THE BUREAUCRACY**

RESULTS
- **THE ARISTOCRACY'S WEALTH & POWER INCREASE**
- **THE 21st CENTURY SERF APPEARS**

Commonsense21c.com

PRODUCTIVITY OF ECONOMIC SYSTEMS:

The thirteenth economics cartoon is the "Productivity of Economic Systems." The cartoon explains how the producers' incentive varies between the Capitalist Economic System and the Tyranny or the Cronyism Economic System. The Cronyism Economic System reduces but does not completely eliminate the producers' incentive.

PRODUCTIVITY OF ECONOMIC SYSTEMS
THE MORE WE PRODUCE, THE BETTER WE LIVE

CAPITALISM
(INDIVIDUAL FREEDOM)

THE PRODUCER

- PRODUCES WEALTH WITH THE EXPECTATION OF BENEFITING FROM THAT WEALTH
- USES INNOVATION TO INCREASE PRODUCTIVITY AND IMPROVE THE STANDARD OF LIVING

TYRANNY
(KINGDOM, COMMUNISM, FASCISM, SOCIALISM, SHEIKDOM, EMPEROR, TRIBAL CHIEF-WITCH DOCTOR etc.)

THE PRODUCER
(21st CENTURY SERF)

- PRODUCES WEALTH FOR THE BENEFIT OF THE ARISTOCRACY
- HAS NO EXPECTATION OF BENEFITTING FROM INCREASED PRODUCTIVITY
- INNOVATION USED TO HIDE WEALTH FROM THE ARISTOCRACY

THE NATION'S "STANDARD OF LIVING" CAN ONLY IMPROVE IF INDIVIDUAL PRODUCTIVITY INCREASES

THE INCOME TAX-AN ECONOMIC BLUNDER:

The cartoon explains why the income tax is a poor choice for the Economy.

THE INCOME TAX – AN ECONOMIC BLUNDER
TAXING INCOME DECREASES PRODUCTIVITY

ARISTOCRACY'S USE OF THE INCOME TAX LAW

- THE ARISTOCRACY'S WEAPON AGAINST THEIR DECLARED ENEMY-THE RICH
- USED TO PUNISH POLITICAL DISSENT
- USED TO REWARD CRONIES & OBTAIN POLITICAL SUPPORT
- COST OF COMPLIANCE TO THE VICTIM MAY EXCEED THE TAX LIABILITY
- COMPLIANCE & ADMINISTRATIVE COSTS ARE LARGE COMPARED TO TAX COLLECTED
- USES ALLEGATIONS OF TAX EVASION AGAINST POLITICAL OPPONENTS

INCOME TAX EFFECTS ON THE ENTREPRENEUR

- REDUCES INCENTIVES
- MAKES FUNDING NEW BUSINESSES DIFFICULT
- COMPLIANCE ADDS SIGNIFICANT START-UP COST TO NEW BUSINESSES
- DISCOURAGES INNOVATION
- PROGRESSIVE INCOME TAX MAKES IT MORE DIFFICULT FOR THE MOST PRODUCTIVE ENTREPRENEURS TO ACCUMULATE CAPITAL TO EXPAND & FUND NEW PRODUCTS

THE GREAT GLOBAL WARMING SCAM:

Never in the field of human endeavor have so few profited so handsomely from expanding poverty throughout the land.

The "Great Global Warming Scam" is an innovative addition to the Aristocracy's agenda. Most of the items in the aristocrat's agenda promise economic favors or advantages over a competitor in return for allowing the Aristocracy to accumulate more power. The "Great Global Warming Scam" eliminates the overhead. The scam only promises to eliminate a fictitious disaster and in return the victims surrender freedom and opportunity. Something for nothing-it doesn't get any better than that! The measures proposed to control or eliminate global warming provide the Aristocracy with a blank check. The power and wealth that the "Great Global Warming Scam" will provide the Aristocracy is unlimited. The account this check is written on is "Prosperity and Freedom."

All of the items necessary to create an economic crisis are proposed to eliminate or control global warming. The economic crisis resulting from the "great global warming scam" may allow the Aristocracy to consolidate its dictatorial powers.

THE GREAT GLOBAL WARMING SCAM:

This cartoon depicts the Aristocracy demanding sacrifice from the people to control or eliminate global warming factitious disaster. The Aristocracy collects the sacrifices and celebrates a profitable addition to their agenda. The Aristocracy brags progress is being made and the contrived disaster will soon be eliminated.

The EPA prepares to attack the "windmill of global warming and instructs the innovator to forget his invention and go tend his mule.

THE EPA'S HOLY GRAIL
THE GREAT GLOBAL WARMING SCAM!
Never in the field of human endeavor have so many worked so hard to expand poverty throughout the land.

GLOBAL WARMING- THE EPA'S HOLY GRAIL

THE EPA (A DON QUIXOTE LOOK-A-LIKE) READY TO ENFORCE THE GREAT GLOBAL WARMING SCAM

- THE WINDMILL SURVIVED THE 1st DON QUIXOTE ATTACK
- WILL THE EPA BE MORE EFFECTIVE?

THE EPA ACTS!

NO

ENTREPRENEUR: "THIS INVENTION WILL CREATE GREAT WEALTH & PROSPERITY"

THE EXTRAVAGANT USE OF ENERGY WILL NOT BE TOLERATED. GO TEND YOUR MULE

Commonsense21c.com

This cartoon illustrates the futility of energy alchemy.

WILL ENERGY ALCHEMY ELIMINATE GLOBAL WARMING?

THE ARISTOCRACY'S ENERGY ALCHEMIST JUSTIFIES ALTERNATIVE ENERGY PROGRAMS

ENERGY ALCHEMIST

- GLOBAL WARMING WILL DESTROY OUR CIVILIZATION
- FOSSIL FUEL CAUSES GLOBAL WARMING
- ENERGY ALCHEMY WILL PROVIDE SOURCES OF AFFORDABLE ENERGY
- ENERGY ALCHEMY WILL PROVIDE AFFORDABLE ENERGY
- OUR PRODUCTIVITY & PROSPERITY WILL BE SALVAGED

GLOBAL WARMING IS A SCAM-FOSSIL FUEL WILL BE THE PRIMARY ENERGY FOR HUNDREDS OF YEARS

ALCHEMY?

MEDIEVAL ALCHEMIST

- DURING MEDIEVAL TIMES THE ALCHEMIST SCAMMED THE KINGS, CLAIMING TO BE ABLE TO CHANGE LEAD INTO GOLD
- TODAY, THE ARISTOCRACY USES THE ENERGY ALCHEMIST'S ALTERNATIVE ENERGY SCAM TO SEIZE WEALTH & POWER

21st CENTURY ALCHEMY-ALTERNATIVE ENERGY?

SOLAR POWER

WIND POWER

Commonsense2lc.com

This cartoon shows wealth used to develop alternative energy sinking into a "black hole."

A media campaign demanding the measures to control global warming be instituted to save the "lovable polar bear cub's habitat.

They neglect to inform the public that the polar bear is one of the most ferocious animals on the planet and one of the few creatures that will stalk man. The fact is that the measures proposed to control the climate will have no effect on the climate.

When one sees this type of propaganda it can only be concluded that the perpetrator's motives must be dishonest.

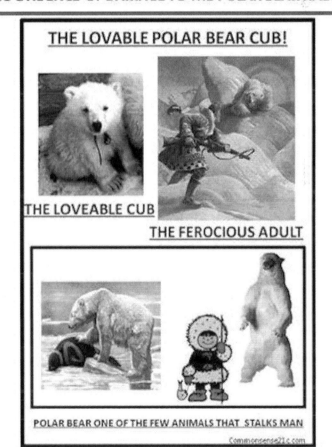

PROSPERITY DEPENDS UPON PRODUCTIVITY:

Increasing our productivity depends upon the unrestricted use of energy to replace our muscles. Will wealth be produced by forty acres and a mule or one thousand acres and a tractor?

PROSPERITY DEPENDS UPON PRODUCTIVITY
PRODUCTIVITY DEPENDS UPON REPLACING MUSCLE ENERGY WITH MECHANICAL ENERGY

MUSCLES   OR   MECHANICAL ENERGY
40 ACRES & A MULE OR 1,000 ACRES & A TRACTOR

- FOSSIL FUEL IS THE ONLY SOURCE OF ECONOMICAL ENERGY LARGE ENOUGH TO SUPPLY SOCIETY'S NEEDS
- ALTERNATIVE ENERGY (ENERGY ALCHEMY) IS BOTH LIMITED & EXPENSIVE. ELIMINATION OF FOSSIL FUEL WILL SEVERELY REDUCE THE STANDARD OF LIVING & REQUIRE STRENUOUS MANUAL LABOR
- THE GREAT GLOBAL WARMING SCAM REQUIRES REDUCTION OR ELIMINATION OF FOSSIL FUEL

THE CHOICE

ENERGY AVAILABLE FOR A PROSPEROUS SOCIETY

POVERTY & DESPAIR CAUSED BY RESTRICTED ENERGY USE TO AVOID A FICTITIOUS DISASTER

THE ARISTOCRACY ASSAULT ON THE CONSTITUTION:

Constitution is quashed!

On February 24, 2011 the Aristocracy proclaimed a Dictatorship. Congress was informed real laws would be ignored (laws that the President is sworn to enforce). The Aristocracy creates illegal new laws with Executive Orders and Bureaucratic regulations. The Aristocracy brags that the "pcn" to solve all of our problems.

The Aristocracy has flawlessly executed a plan to create a nation of slaves slowly reinstating the tyranny of King George III, but under new management!

When the Aristocracy creates new "laws" with its pen, Congress is irrelevant!

The next six cartoons are in this section.

This cartoon shows the Aristocracy ignoring the Constitution and converting the citizens to "21st Century Serfs."

DEATH OF THE REPUBLIC
FEBRUARY, 4, 2011

THE ARISTOCRACY DECLARES A DICTATORSHIP

ONLY SELECTED LAWS WILL BE ENFORCED.
EXECUTIVE ORDERS ARE NOW THE "LAW OF THE LAND"

SLAVERY IS REINSTATED AS THE 21st CENTURY SERF!

DUTIES OF THE PRESIDENT LISTED IN UNITED STATES CONSTITUTION.
ARTICLE. II, SECTION.3.
"He shall take Care that the Laws be faithfully executed"

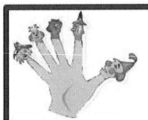

THE PUPPET PRESS TELLS US THAT IT IS RACIST TO OPPOSE THIS SLAVERY

Commonsense21c.com

ARISTOCRACY QUASHES THE CONSTITUTION:

This cartoon lists the Aristocracy's violations of the Constitution and the effects of those offenses on the Republic.

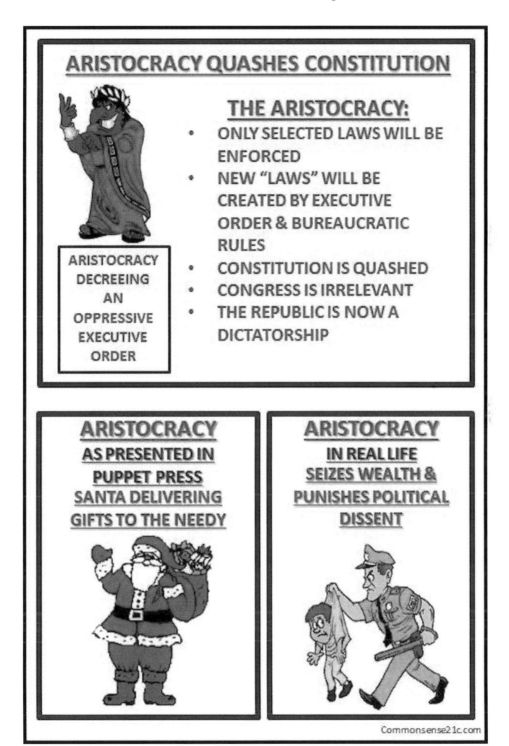

AMENDING THE CONSTITUTION:

Amending the Constitution requires approval of ¾ of the states. Now five (5) Supreme Court Justices change the meaning of the Constitution at will? Was this the intent of the founding Fathers? During the 2000 Presidential champagne, Mr. Gores said we have a **"LIVING BREATHING CONSTITUTION."** A **"LIVING BREATHING CONSTITUTION"** is no Constitution at all!

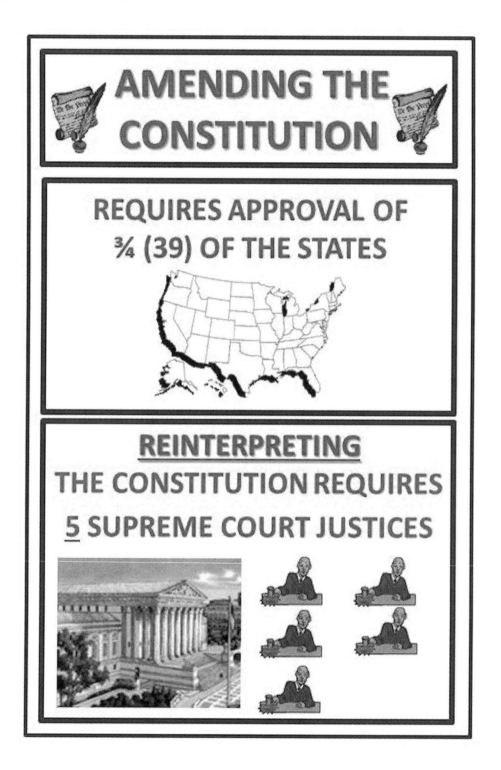

THE CONSTITUTION & THE COURTS:

The courts can change the Constitution simply by reinterpreting the meaning.

Will the Aristocracy become the source of laws or will Congress prevail?

HOW WILL LAWS BE ENACTED?

AN ARISTOCRACY
THAT SIGNS AWAY YOUR RIGHTS & CONFISCATES YOUR WEALTH WITH A STROKE OF A PEN

OR

THE CONSTITUTION
Article. I.
Section. 1.
All legislative Powers herein granted shall be vested in a Congress of the United States, which shall consist of a Senate and House of Representatives.

Commonsense21c.com

Can the Aristocracy enact legal laws with the stroke of a pen? The Constitution says no!

ARE EXECUTIVE ORDERS LAWS?
WHO DO YOU BELIEVE?

THE FOUNDING FATHERS

THE CONSTITUTION

ARTICLE I

SECTION I

All legislative powers granted shall be vested in the Congress of the United States, which shall consist of a Senate and House of Representatives.

OR

THE ARISTOCRACY

"The Constitution constrains me"

That's the same argument that both Hitler & Mussolini used to justify Dictatorial powers!

Commonsense21c.com

THE ARISTOCRACY'S ACHILLES HEEL:

Veterans, the military and police organizations are sworn to defend the Constitution. Is that the Aristocracy's Achilles Heel?

THE ARISTOCRACY'S ACHILLES HEEL

THE MILITARY AND VETERANS OF THE MILITARY ARE SWORN TO DEFEND THE CONSTITUTION AGAINST ALL ENEMIES, BOTH FOREIGN & DOMESTIC

IF THE ARISTOCRACY VIOLATES THE CONSTITUTION, IT IS THE SWORN DUTY OF THESE PATRIOTS (BOTH MILITARY, VETERANS & POLICE ORGANIZATIONS) TO DEFEND OUR CONSTITUTION

THE ARISTOCRACY:
WE ARE NOT LIMITED
BY THE CONSTITUTION

COULD THE OATH TAKEN BY THE MILITARY BE THE REASON THE ARISTOCRACY'S TRYING TO LABEL VETERANS AS TERRORISTS, PURGING HIGH RANKING MILITARY LEADERS & TRYING TO CONFUSE THE ACTUAL MEANING OF THE CONSTITUTION?

JUDGE:
THE CONSTITUTION
IS WHAT I SAY IT IS

THE ARISTOCRACY'S PUPPET PRESS-SECTION:

This section contains four cartoons that comment on the Puppet Press's mandate. The Puppet Press distributes the propaganda for the Aristocracy and suppresses the truth.

1st PRIORITY OF THE ARISTOCRACY:

The Puppet Press is the first priority on the Aristocracy. This cartoon presents the mandate of the Puppet Press.

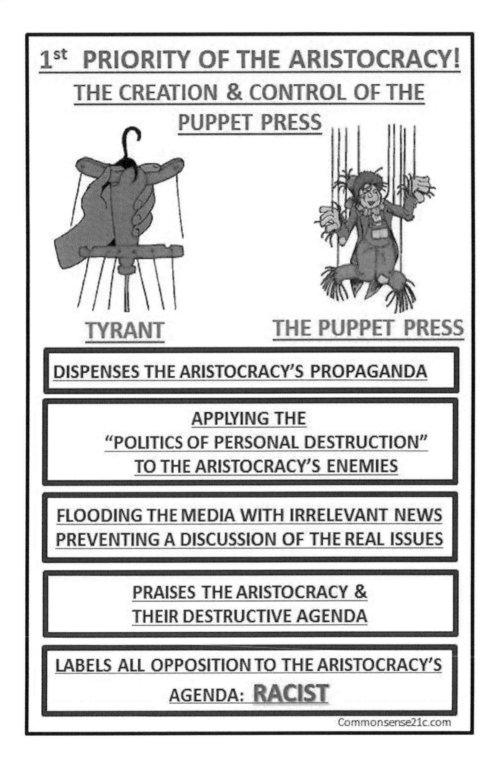

FACE THE MUSIC!

The second Puppet Press cartoon tells you to face the music with the Aristocracy's orchestra and shows the Aristocracy's control over the media.

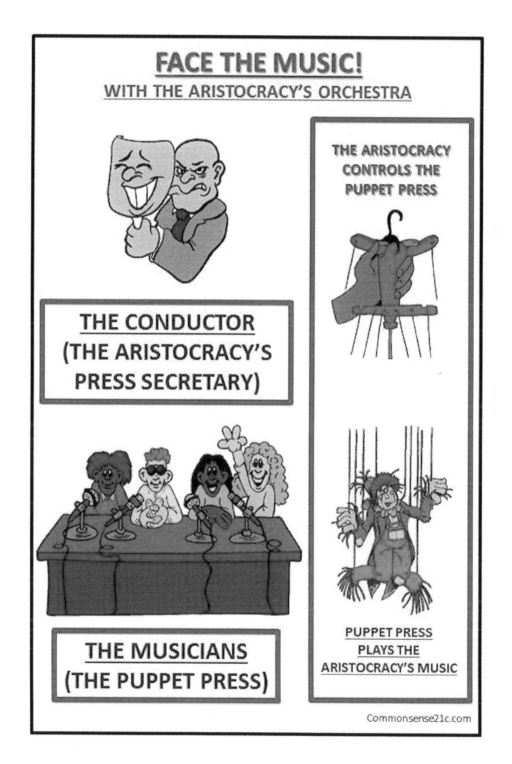

PROPAGANDA CAN BE DANGEROUS:

This cartoon demonstrates that propaganda can be dangerous when the teleprompter malfunctions.

THE PROPAGANDA MACHINE:

The cartoon defines the Puppet Press as the Aristocracy's propaganda machine and quotes Mr. Hitler and Mr. Goebbels on the value of propaganda to the Aristocracy.

THE PROPAGANDA MACHINE

THE PUPPET PRESS-THE ARISTOCRACY'S CH0IR
DISPENSES THE ARISTOCRACY'S PROPAGANDA &
BLOCKS OR MANIPULATES THE OPPOSITION'S MESSAGE

COMMENTS ON PROPAGANDA FROM HISTORICAL USERS

ADOLF HITLER :
- "BY THE SKILLFUL AND SUSTAINED USE OF PROPAGANDA, ONE CAN MAKE A PEOPLE SEE EVEN HEAVEN AS HELL OR AN EXTREMELY WRETCHED LIFE AS PARADISE."

JOSEPH GOEBBELS:
- "THINK OF THE PRESS AS A GREAT KEYBOARD ON WHICH THE GOVERNMENT CAN PLAY."

PROPAGANDA IS CONTROL & MANIPULATION OF INFORMATION FOR THE BENEFIT OF THE ARISTOCRACY

Commonsense21c.com

THE BIPARTISAN SECTION:

This section is concerned with Bipartisan Politics. The Puppet Press has glorified the term "bipartisan" declaring it to be a virtue. Bipartisanship occurs when the opposition party renounces its values and supports the Aristocracy's agenda. The purpose of the Aristocracy's agenda is the accumulation of power and wealth at the expense of the people. A bipartisan effort that succeeded in implementing that agenda would be devastating to the Republic. Glorifying the tern "bipartisan" is just more propaganda by the Puppet Press seeking to advance the Aristocracy's agenda.

There are three cartoons in the Bipartisan section.

BIPARTISAN POLITICS:

This cartoon explains the real meaning of the term "bipartisan" and the devastating results if the Republican Party actually adopted that policy. The Republican Party should research the "Night of the Long Knives" before deciding to become bipartisan.

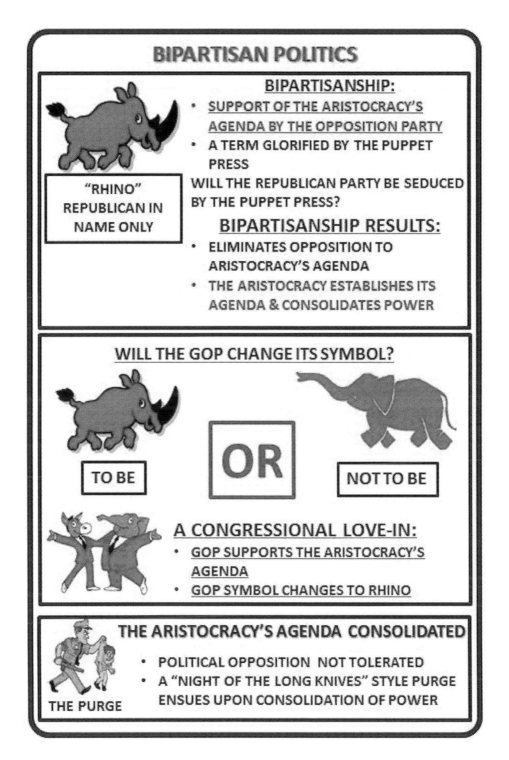

A CONGRESSIONAL LOVE-IN:

This cartoon adds more on the meaning and consequences of a bipartisan policy.

A CONGRESSIONAL LOVE-IN

BIPARTISANSHIP

CONGRESSIONAL LOVE-IN

- BIPARTISANSHIP - THE OPPOSITION PARTY SUPPORTS THE ARISTOCRACY'S AGENDA
- THE ARISTOCRACY IMPOSES ITS AGENDA, WITHOUT OPPOSITION
- THE ARISTOCRACY BECOMES A DICTATORSHIP

EXPLOITED CITIZEN

"NO MAN'S LIFE, LIBERTY OR PROPERTY ARE SAFE WHILE THE LEGISLATURE IS IN SESSION."
QUOTE FROM
Gideon J. Tucker, 1826

A BIPARTISAN CONGRESS REMOVES ALL RESTRAINT!

ARISTOCRACY

- CELEBRATES THE CONSOLIDATION OF POWER
- PURGES THE OPPOSITION- REENACTING HITLER'S "NIGHT OF THE LONG KNIVES"

THE DICTATORSHIP IS COMPLETE

This cartoon is another explanation of the consequences of a bipartisan policy.

THE MISCELLANEOUS SECTION:

This section contains cartoons that do not fit in the other sections. It is not that these cartoons are less important there are just too few cartoons on each subject to justify a section.

There are five cartoons in this section.

The armed Patriot is the last defense against the Aristocracy. When the Puppet Press has confused most of the people and an economic crisis grips the economy, the last hope for the Republic is the armed Patriot.

This cartoon displays the consequences of disarming the patriot.

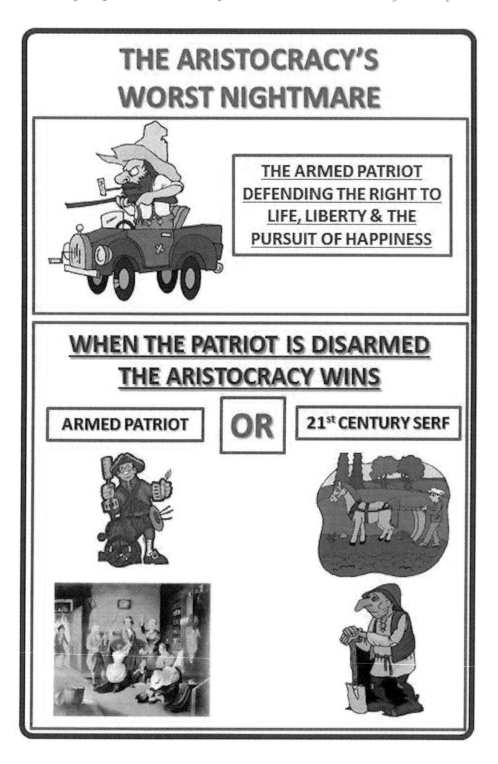

THE 3 GREATEST DANGERS TO THE REPUBLIC:

This cartoon describes the three greatest dangers to the Republic.

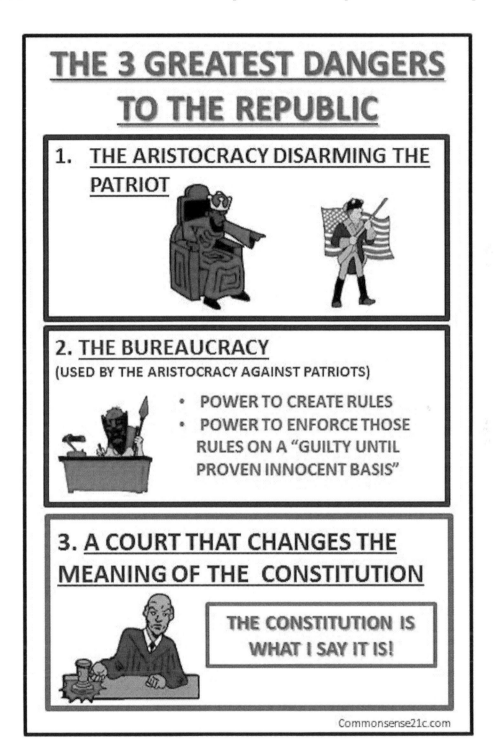

THE PELOSI LEGACY:

Ms. Pelosi forced a vote on the Obama Care legislation before she allowed the Congress access to the content of that legislation. She said that "we have to pass this quickly so that we can find out what's in it." Are we in the hands of raving lunatics?

THE PELOSI LEGACY
WITHHOLDING THE CONTENT OF LEGISLATION FROM THE CONGRESS UNTIL AFTER IT IS ENACTED INTO LAW

MS. PELOSI

MS. PELOSI:
"WE HAVE TO PASS IT QUICKLY SO THAT WE CAN FIND OUT WHAT'S IN IT"

KING GEORGE III

- ONE OF THE GRIEVANCES AGAINST KING GEORGE III WAS "TAXATION WITHOUT REPRESENTATION."
- ITS WORSE WITH MS. PELOSI <u>WE HAVE REPRESENTATIVES BUT NO REPRESENTATION</u>

DELETE THE PELOSI LEGACY
AMEND THE CONSTITUTION TO REQUIRE CONGRESSPERSONS TO PASS A QUIZ ON THE CONTENT OF A LAW BEFORE THEY ARE ALLOWED TO VOTE

THIS ADMINISTRATION:

Since its inception, this Administration has been rocked by scandals that would have brought down any other Administration in the history of our country. The most grievous scandal is the Internal Revenue Services (IRS) attacking Aristocracy's enemies. Both Mr. Roosevelt and Mr. Nixon use of the IRS to attack political enemies to this this scandal. This Administration's cover-up of the scandal would not have tolerated during the Nixon Administration.

The administration claimed no prior knowledge of any of these scandals until the scandals became public knowledge.

So far, The IRS has successfully covered up the scandal. This cover-up would never have been allowed during the Nixon administration.

Where is the outrage?

Where is the demand for an Independent Special Counsel?

The Puppet Press is truly the handmaiden of the Aristocracy!

THIS ADMINISTRATION

- SCANDALS & BLUNDERS HAVE PLAGUED THIS ADMINISTRATION SINCE ITS INCEPTION
- THE ADMINISTRATION DENIED ANY PRIOR KNOWLEDGE OF THESE FIASCOS
- THE MOST GRIEVOUS OF THESE HUMILIATIONS WAS THE IRS ATTACK ON THE ARISTOCRACY'S ENEMIES & THE ENSUING COVER-UP

IS THIS ADMINISTRATION LYING OR IS IT JUST INCOMPETENT?

AN ARISTOCRACY
GUILTY OF OPPRESSING POLITICAL DISSENT

OR

AN INCOMPETENT CLOWN
THE VICTIM OF AN OUT-OF-CONTROL BUREAUCRACY

MALICE OR INCOMPETENCE? WHICH POSES THE GREATER THREAT?

Commonsense21c.com

EPILOGUE:

The purpose of this book was to simplify the Aristocracy's agenda and highlight the inconsistencies in Aristocracy's arguments supporting that agenda. Since the adoption of the Constitution, it has been the goal of the Aristocracy to undermine the rights guaranteed to the individual by that document. For almost 100 years the Aristocracy's agenda was stalled. In 1888 Congress created the Interstate Commerce Commission (ICC) and revived Aristocracy's agenda. Since 1888, the Aristocracy's agenda has enjoyed slow but continuous implementation.

The gains in human rights facilitated by the American Revolution have been almost wiped out. We are approaching the "point of no return." The Aristocracy's agenda has laid the groundwork to create an economic crisis. That economic crisis may well facilitate the Aristocracy's Dictatorship.

Aristocracy has almost reinstated the tyranny of King George III under new management. May God have mercy on our souls!

BOOKS BY FELTON WILLIAMSON, JR.

"21st CENTURY COMMON SENSE"

Explains how we have allowed the Aristocracy to destroy our flawed capitalistic system and replace it with the tyranny of King George III, under new management. The disastrous results of the Aristocracy's five highly touted programs:

- The Income Tax Laws
- Inflation
- Antitrust Laws
- Earmarks
- The Bureaucracy

Included in the book are the economic advantages of the "Technology Dividend", the greatest threat to our Republic, and a recipe to regain our freedom and prosperity are included.

"COMMON SENSE THE WAY BACK"

An abridged version of "21st CENTURY COMMON SENSE"

"THE TEA PARTY & THE TYRANT"

A group of articles describing the conflict between the Tea Party and the Aristocracy

"TOBY'S FABLE"

A short fictional account of how the Bureaucracy abuses its victims, maintains the status quo, and increases everyone's cost of living.

"Cartoons of Coercion"

"CARTOONS OF COERCION" is a collection of 40 outrageous cartoons. If a picture is worth 1000 words, the 40 cartoons in "Cartoons of Coercion" contain a lot of material for a book with only 5,000 words of text. This is not a book you read; you just enjoy the pictures.

Short sections of text explain the purpose of and conditions that led to the creation of these cartoons.

Each of the illustrations is listed in the Table of Contents and may be accessed by clicking on the title of the illustration in the Kindle Edition. In the print edition, the page of each cartoon is listed. The purpose of this format is to allow the reader to easily use the Kindle, iPod or other device to show specific cartoons to a friend.

Proof

Made in the USA
Charleston, SC
04 August 2014